# VENUS AND SERENA WILLIAMS

## DISCOVER THE LIFE OF A SPORTS STAR

David and Patricia Armentrout

Rourke

Publishing LLC
Vero Beach, Florida 32964

www.rourkepublishing.com

PHOTO CREDITS: All photos © Getty Images

Title page: *Serena and Venus have both played tennis since they were very young.*

Editor: Frank Sloan

Cover and interior design by Nicola Stratford

## Library of Congress Cataloging-in-Publication Data

Armentrout, David, 1962-
  Venus and Serena Williams / David and Patricia Armentrout.
    v. cm. -- (Discover the life of a sports star)
Includes bibliographical references and index.
Contents: Star sisters -- A father's guidance -- Venus -- Serena -- Time for a change -- Going pro -- Spotlight on Venus -- Spotlight on Serena -- Champion sisters.
  ISBN 1-58952-655-4 (hardcover)
  1. Williams, Venus, 1980---Juvenile literature. 2. Williams, Serena, 1981---Juvenile literature. 3. Tennis players--United States--Biography--Juvenile literature. 4. African American women tennis players--Biography--Juvenile literature. [1. Williams, Venus 1980- 2. Williams, Serena, 1981- 3. Tennis players. 4. African Americans--Biography. 5. Women--Biography.] I. Armentrout, Patricia, 1960- II. Title. III. Series:  Armentrout, David, 1962-   Discover the life of a sports star.
  GV994.A1A74 2003
  796.342'092'2--dc21
                         2003005935

Printed in the USA
CG/CG

# Table of Contents

*Serena and Venus won the gold medal for the Women's Doubles in the 2000 Olympics.*

# Star Sisters

Venus and Serena Williams are two of the best-known athletes in the world. They are stars in the world of tennis. Every time they step onto the court they take the game of tennis by storm.

**Venus:**
Born 1980, turned pro 1994
**Serena:**
Born 1981, turned pro 1995
**Records:** Multiple titles each, including Doubles Champions at the 2003 Australian Open

# A Father's Guidance

Venus and Serena grew up loving the game of tennis, thanks to their father, Richard. Richard always wanted his girls to become tennis stars. He did everything in his power to make that dream come true.

Richard became the girls' coach, teaching them everything they needed to know about tennis. Oracene, the girls' mother, supported the girls and Richard's coaching methods every step of the way.

*Richard Williams coached and supported his daughters as they became tennis stars.*

*Venus spent **hours** practicing tennis as a young girl.*

# Venus

Venus was born June 17, 1980. Venus is 15 months older than Serena and was handed a tennis racket first. Almost instantly, Venus was able to pop balls over the net with ease.

By the time she was six, Venus was studying and imitating the top tennis stars on television. At ten, she thought she could be number one. Venus was strong and confident, and she loved the game.

*Serena quickly learned the skills that would make her a great tennis player.*

# Serena

Serena was born September 26, 1981. Serena watched as her older sister practiced. She couldn't wait to play tennis, too. When Serena was able to join her sister on the courts, she took to the game right away. She immediately showed her **competitive** spirit.

Over the next few years the girls played in several age-group **tournaments**, and they won many games.

*The Williams family moved to Florida to focus on tennis.*

# Time for a Change

In 1991, Mr. Williams decided it was time for a change. He wanted his girls to get **professional** instruction.

The family moved from California to Florida. The girls no longer competed in junior tournaments. Instead, they learned by playing against older, stronger, adult pros. Venus grew into a world-class player, and in 1994, at the age of 14, she decided to go pro.

# Going Pro

Venus entered her first Women's Tennis Association (WTA) tournament in 1994. She surprised everyone with her strong **serves**. She played well and won her first two **sets**. But she lost her third set to the second ranked player in the world, Arantxa Sanchez Vicario.

Meanwhile, Serena was also becoming quite a competitor. She developed a style all her own and turned pro in 1995.

*Serena and Venus make an awesome pair in doubles competition.*

# Spotlight on Venus

Venus is known for her overwhelming serves. She clocked a women's world record in 1998 with a 127-mile (204-kilometer) an hour serve. Venus also uses incredible force in every shot, which forces her opponents always to be on the defensive.

Venus played her first U.S. Open in 1997. In 1998 and 1999 Venus won the Singles title at the Lipton Championships. Venus and Serena teamed up to win the Doubles championship in 1999 at the French Open and U.S. Open.

*Venus returns the ball during the 1999 U.S. Open match in New York.*

*Serena returns the ball to Lindsay Davenport during a 1999 U.S. Open match.*

# Spotlight on Serena

Serena is smaller than Venus, but she is equally athletic. She uses smooth, consistent strokes with great force. Serena is good at spotting flaws in her opponent's game, and she will change strategy in the middle of a match if necessary.

Serena won the Singles title at the U.S. Open in 1999. Serena and Venus teamed up again and won the Doubles at Wimbledon in 2000.

# Champion Sisters

Venus won the Singles title at Wimbledon and the U.S. Open and the Doubles **Grand Slam** Trophy with Serena in Australia in 2001.

Serena won the Singles title at Wimbledon and her second Grand Slam title at the French Open in 2002, defeating her sister Venus. At the Australian Open in January 2003 Serena slammed Venus to win the Singles title, and both were crowned Doubles champions.

*Venus and Serena celebrate their Doubles Championship at the 2003 Australian Open.*

# Dates to Remember

1980    Venus is born June 17 in Lynwood, California

1981    Serena is born September 26 in Saginaw, Michigan

1998    Venus wins her first Singles title; Serena plays her first Grand Slam event in Australia

1999    Doubles Champs for Venus and Serena at French and Australian Open

2000    Venus wins Singles at Wimbledon and U.S. Open and Doubles at Wimbledon with Serena

2001    Venus and Serena win Doubles at the Australian Open; Venus wins Singles at the Wimbledon and the U.S. Open

2002    Serena wins Singles at French and Wimbledon Open and Doubles with Venus at Wimbledon

2003    Serena wins Singles at the Australian Open and Doubles with Venus

# Glossary

**competitive** (cum PET uh tiv) — able to play with great skill

**Grand Slam** (GRAND SLAM) — one of the four major tournaments played once a year—Australian Open, French Open, Wimbledon, U.S. Open

**professional** (pruh FESH uh nuhl) — a paid instructor or player

**serves** (SURVZ) — beginning play by tossing the ball into the air and hitting it with the racket over the net into the service court diagonally opposite; serve is determined by flipping a coin and a player serves for the entire game

**sets** (SETS) — a set is winning six games before an opponent wins four games

**tournaments** (TUR nuh muhntz) — a series of contests where a number of players try to win the championship

# Index

## Further Reading

Christopher, Matt. *On the Court with Venus and Serena Williams*. Little Brown &
    Company, 2002.
Gutman, Bill. *Venus & Serena: The Grand Slam Williams Sisters*. Scholastic Inc., 2001.
Stewart, Mark. *Venus & Serena Williams: Sisters in Arms*. Millbrook Press, 2000.

## Websites To Visit

www.usopen.org/
www.wtastarz.com/

## About The Authors

David and Patricia Armentrout have written many nonfiction books for young readers.
They have had several books published for primary school reading. The Armentrouts
live in Cincinnati, Ohio, with their two children.